How to Overcome Every Objection: Six Words That Convert Objections to Conversations

Category: Business & Economics

Author: Bob Oros

Publisher: Bob Oros Publishing

ISBN: 978-1-387-20117-4

Copyright 2017

Description: If you show a genuine concern for their objections they will feel appreciated and will be willing to continue. If they made up the objection they will feel bad and will consider your services even more. The worst approach to objections is to get defensive. You cannot get upset at a client for any reason.

Key words: sales techniques, job in sales, sales manager training, manufacturing sales training, wholesale sales training, distributor sales training, food service sales, sales coaching, motivating sales people, sales course, overcome objections, food sales jobs,

ISBN 978-1-387-20117-4

9 781387 201174

1. How to overcome every objection

It is easier for a person to stay with what they are doing, even if they are not completely satisfied, than it is to risk a change.

Why will someone continue to buy from a sales person when it is obvious they are not happy with the service, price or quality? The reason is that the buyer is comfortable dealing with the sales person and company he or she is buying from. To make a change requires assurances that you will be able to handle their business. Many times in the buyers mind it is easier to stay with their current supplier even if the prices and delivery are not exactly as they would like. That is why they have at least five objections that you must overcome before they feel sure enough to give you their business.

The best response to smoke screen objections is to be sincerely glad they brought it up. When answering "smoke screen" objections the normal response is to agree with the objection, however, the best response is to say "I'm glad you brought that up!" And then ask a question.

This is a non confrontational approach. When you do it sincerely you will come across with real concern for your customer.

How would you handle these common objections?

I have too many suppliers already.

I really don't like your company.

We've been doing all right without you.

I'm tied up in a supplier contract.

I'm happy with my present supplier.

You don't carry a full line.

I'm not interested at this time.

See me in a couple of months.

I hear your company is having problems.

Business is down.

When answering these "smoke screen" objections the normal response is to agree with the objection, however, an excellent response is to say "I'm glad you brought that up!" And then ask a question. For example:

"I don't like your company". Response: "I'm glad you brought that up. It sounds to me like someone must have done something in the past and it is Important that we get honest feedback about our products and services. What exactly is it that you don't like about our company?"

"I have too many suppliers already". Response: "I'm glad you brought that up. That certainly can be a problem, how many is too many?" "I may be able to help you consolidate," etc.

"You don't carry the items I need". Response: "I'm glad you brought that up. would you mind telling me which items you are referring to?"

Often we can get the prospect to answer his own objection or to admit that it is not a valid objection. To let the prospect answer his own objection you just let them talk. Perhaps this is all he wants to do anyway. So ask your prospect questions about his objections and let him talk. Maybe he will answer his own argument. In any event, he will lower his blood pressure.

You may say, for example, "I am interested in why you say that, Mr. Smith. I wish you would explain it to me more fully." You may merely ask him, "Why do you believe that?" If, as so often happens, the objection is not a valid one and the prospect has at best only a half-baked idea of what he is talking about, he will usually flounder around a while and end by admitting that the matter is of no importance.

Comments:

This is a good list to refer back to when addressing these kinds of objections. I think that most people hear comments like that from potential customers and completely shut down. You know its natural to hear something that negative and to think in the back for your mind, "There's just no way this person is going to do business with me." It is a good idea to make a mental note of some of these responses as well as practice responses to those kinds of questions because you will really catch them of guard when you a fluid response to the objections.

Drew Culbreth

I like the idea of influencing the client to explain an objection they are having. This goes back to the idea that we are business consultants rather than salesmen. If we show a genuine concern for their objections they will feel appreciated and will be willing to spill the beans. If they made up the objection they will feel bad and will consider your services even more. The worst approach to objections is to get defensive. You cannot get upset at a client for any reason. You will not make a sale if you set a negative mood.

Cullin Hamm

This is an area that I probably need more practice in. I am not always sure that I ask the correct questions when someone gives me an objection. I may tend to agree with them and then after I have left the customer I think, "Why didn't I ask this or that." This occurs mainly on a sales call that I may not feel "within my comfort zone." You know there are some customers that just tend to make you a little more nervous than others. This is an area that I work on daily. I will tell you it is much better than the first two weeks I started selling. Boy, were they bad as far as my nerves go. I'd drive around the block a half dozen times working up my nerve. That sounds funny now. But it wasn't then. I will work on asking more questions if they try to give me the "smoke screen routine."

Patsy Clements

It is always helpful to have suggestions on how to handle the smoke screens. The one I get, and I am to assume it is true is that business is slow. I think some of the company's automatically come up with smoke screens hoping not to make commitments.

Pam High

Sincerely ask why? If you ask why and show that you truly want to know what the reasoning for the objection is. The truth of the objective will come to light. It might be that the company does have a problem that you could help solve. Or it might be that you have forced them to move on to another subject since called them out on the problem.

Christal Cornacchia

The point is, if they don't want to buy from you, you can't force them. Being prepared and not being too impatient is important. You must keep an ongoing relationship with the client, whether you close or not. You never know what day will be your day to close with a particular client. Always be ready!!

Kimberly Burgess

Those darn smoke screen objections. They are so common what it really means is "I don't want to be bothered. You're just a slimy salesperson out to get my money!" Well that's how I feel about them, now I know how to handle them a little better or at least continue the conversation a minute or two longer!

Morgan Frazier

2. How can a customer buy insurance against failure?

A professional sales person knows exactly what to do when a prospect keeps harping away on nothing but "Your price is too high" when trying to present a higher quality product.

Simply ask: "How much too high, Mr. Brown?" This immediately stops the prospect. First of all, it puts him on the defensive - where he thought he had put you - and second, it forces him to elaborate on his simple statement, "Your price is too high." He may then say something like this: "Your price is 10% higher than Jones - and if I can save 10% under our new cost-cutting program, I've got to do it. Now you can go to work. Now you have something to take hold of. You can focus on the difference, not the price. Paying 10% more for quality is an investment or insurance, never an expense. Everyone can remember making a purchase based on a low price that we later regretted.

No matter how hard you worked or how many concessions you have made when you sell a customer, he or she still feels that you owe them a favor. Do you know what your customer expects after the sale?

The perception on the part of the customer is that you, the seller, have not only gotten new business but also his or her money. There are many other sales people after the same account and the same business but you were chosen as the recipient. Therefore, psychologically, you now owe your customer a favor. Even though you had to bend over backwards to get the order. That is why follow up is so important to keeping the business.

You have been calling on a particular customer for months and have never gotten to first base. They are polite, however, they keep telling you to come back at a later date.

All of a sudden you make a small sale! As soon as you leave the account you check the stock status. Everything is checked and you drop a card in the mail that your customer receives the next morning confirming the order, delivery date and approximate delivery time. After you check to be sure everything was delivered you make a follow up call to be sure everything was alright with the product. You get a few small reorders and continue the same follow up strategies. And then the orders get larger. Soon you are the primary supplier. Later you are having lunch with the customer and he lets you in on the reason he switched: YOU FOLLOWED UP AND YOUR COMPETITOR DID NOT!

This meticulous follow up that you do is YOUR insurance policy against failure, just as your customers insurance is to buy a product or service that will do the job.

Comments:

Although there are no guarantees against failure, I have found persistence and follow up always pay off. Sometimes a prospect is unable to give you the business but will recommend you to a friend or company.

Paulette Clarke

Never promise something in a sale you can't produce. I believe being honest and following up and delivering on your promises to a client is the best way to build insurance with a new client.

Heath Blanchard

I have always been very proud of the companies I have worked for. Therefore I have no problem letting the client know that our price is higher because we have a lot to offer. I always explain to the client "If you don't like our service, then by all means don't use us." I want to make sure I am offering them the best level of customer service that they have ever experienced.

I know this may sound harsh, but it works. It lets the client know that you believe in what you are selling. The article discussed being in front of the client. Make sure you are working with your planner. It always helps to maintain contact. The client will remember when that other agency isn't cutting it!! Pleasantly persistent but not annoying.

Danah Parmley

To insure that our customer can depend on us we must have excellent customer service at all time. One way we provide this is by constant follow ups. We do follow ups with each and every customer on weekly basis and sometimes on a daily basis depending on there current needs. It doesn't matter if it is a new customer or one that we have been doing business with for years. You must always follow up on the day to day business to insure success. We strive daily to find ways to help serve each customer better.

Laura Arnett

Yes this sounds like the recipe for a sound business practice, simple, easy to do, but rarely done! We tend to move to the next prospect forgetting about the small client we just gained and could lose at a moments notice!

Morgan Frazier

Buying quality is certainly one way to buy security. Selling quality is also one way to ensure that the customer will be looking for increased support. Here's where the 'you owe me a favour' train of thought kicks in. The fact is, it is almost always easier to give that support to a loyal customer who buys the quality. I am happy to include the service as much as I can. Following up can assist with customer retention, it will also likely assist with advertising via word of mouth. Happy customers like to brag about the deal they got on their $10 000 stove - the deal is the service.

Wendy Parrott

I don't think you can buy insurance on failure. We deal with the most unpredictable product on the planet.... the human being. What we can do is not fail ourselves. We must be efficient, proficient, and dedicated to what we should be doing and that is, to build long lasting relationships with our large customers and do our job to the satisfaction of our one time, temporary customers, because you never know where the people in one business might move around and be in the future.

Drew Culbreth

3. How important is recognition to your customers?

Even the person who brushes it off as being unimportant has within them a natural desire to be recognized. If you sent a greeting card to 10 people you know with only one word on it - CONGRATULATIONS - at least 8 of them would believe they did something to be recognized for.

There are many ways to give a customer recognition. It can be tied in to anything that is important to your company:

"Customer of the year"

"Largest order"

"First order"

"New item purchased"

"Customer since 1902".

The important point to keep in mind is not to wait for the end of the year, or for your company to come up with a program. Be creative and do something on your own.

It doesn't take long to take business away from a sales person who foolishly take their customers for granted. Most of the time when we call on new or prospective accounts we feel like we are bothering them or causing them some type of inconvenience. Because of this feeling we sometimes convince ourselves that it is not necessary to make the call. Just the opposite is true. Most people like to be called on by sales people. Many times their current suppliers are neglecting them, taking the business for granted. By making the call and giving them the attention that may be missing, leaves the door wide open.

Whenever targeting a new account, the best approach is to contact the daylights of them. Call them for any reason at all. Write letters. Send clippings. Take an aggressive approach and rush them half to death. It works. There is a tendency for a sales person to let up once they have the business.

Animal trainers pet and reward their animals with delicacies for acts of obedience. Children respond with joy when they are given recognition. Even vegetation grows better for those who love it.

No one seems to know Just how praise and recognition releases energy. But the fact that it does is common experience. Ever notice how, when someone pays you a sincere compliment, or thanks you for a job well done, your spirits seem to get a shot in the arm?

The lift that you get from recognition is not an illusion. Neither is it just your imagination. In some way, unknown to science, actual physical energy is released.

Recognition and appreciation is even more powerful when the person does not expect it, or necessarily feel that he or she deserves it. Think back to some time when you got a nice "thank you" from someone where it never occurred to you that any "thanks" were in order and you'll see what I mean.

Comments:

In a world in which we are so busy prospecting, identifying, proposing, and trying to close sales, I think it is imperative that we step back and remember those that have gotten us where we are and show them how much they are valued. Sometimes, I think, we get so busy trying to show potential clients how much we appreciate them in trying to "win their business", that we tend to forget about those that are actually doing business with us daily. That makes no sense!!! Everyone has the need to know they

are valued, lets not mistakenly think that the clients that have earned our thanks and respect..... already know.

Bill Hatfield

Customers are people too. Just like us, we are looking for Recognition as well. So you know when you do something good, you want to be recognized. So now, put yourself in the customers position. To show the customers how appreciation you are of them, it is very important you let them know. Calling or dropping by to say some kind words will go a long way. You have to be look after your business, make sure the competition is not going come and take your business away.

Jim Harris

Recognition doesn't even have to be something tangible. Most people consider recognition to be a trinket, a card, a freebie of some sort, but surprisingly a thank you phone call can do just as much. Even if you need to leave a voicemail to your customers know that you appreciate their business, it can leave quite the impression. Take 2 minutes, and call one customer a day, and before you know it, you will have called every contact, and they will feel like you gave them recognition, something that does not come along every day.

Laura J. Czajka

I am guilty of having these kinds of withdrawals about calling on certain customers because I can relate to how busy can be at time. But by showing the respect they deserve for the value of their time it is a good way to set up appointments in the future. Recognizing that a person is important and that you are willing to base your schedule around them because of the fact that you understand how important their time is, is an opportunity in your grasp.

Drew Culbreth

NEVER TAKE YOUR CLIENTS FOR GRANTED! Remember, clients want praise, recognition, and glory for giving you the business as much as you want praise, recognition and glory for earning their business.

Scott Green

Recognition is very important to you and your clients. You must show your customers how much it means to you and your business. If you don't let your customers know how much they are appreciated they can fell like they are being used. We all need to here how much we are appreciated or needed. Call your customers and take them out for lunch and let them know that there not just another client. We need to be appreciated both when you are doing an outstanding job and when things aren't going so great.

Laura Rice

Most people recognize their clients at the end of the year, but I think it would have more of an effect if it was done at a different time. Your clients would not be expecting anything say at the one year anniversary of their first order or if you sent them a birthday card. We just need to let our clients know that we appreciate them and want to keep their business.

Suzanne Bennett

Very important! No one likes to feel unappreciated or taken for granted. The element of surprise with creativity thrown in, will make a lasting impression on the customer. Like kids, everyone remembers the unexpected treats.

Paulette Clarke

It is always important to let your customer that their business means the world to us. I like how our invoice templates say "Thank you for your business" – which means every week we are thanking our customers.

It keeps relations and rapport positive and enhances the working relationship when your customers know that they matter to you. We like to tell our best customers how much our employees enjoy their work environment and how pleasant they are to work with. We usually get reciprocal feedback. It's also a sales tool. If your customer knows that you value them, and of course they value you, then use them as a reference when you are selling. We have a lot of offices in small towns where everyone knows everyone and good word of mouth gets around fast.

Marquesa Ortega

Recognition to your customers has to be genuine and sincere in order for it to be effective. It is very hard to recognize all of your customers but is a crucial step in maintaining your current clientele. I have been updating all of my customer's agreements for the last couple of weeks. It gives me an opportunity to acknowledge them as being a very important customer. I hand out note pads and pens and make sure they know I appreciate their business. It is important to do the small things for customers in order to gain their loyalty. Let me rephrase that. A small thing to you, such as a thank you card can make a huge difference to your customer.

Cullin Hamm

4. How can you overcome telephone reluctance?

Overcome telephone call reluctance. Use the telephone as a tool to become more cost effective.

The average cost of a personal visit by a sales rep has more than doubled in the past ten years. Time management, carefully prepared sales presentations and making firm appointments for new account calls now have a new meaning.

Working without a schedule, making unprepared calls, spending too much time on marginal or unprofitable accounts, taking too many small orders and not making good use of the telephone are just a few of the old habits that do not work any more.

Efficiency is the ability to do the greatest amount of work with the least possible amount of effort, in the shortest period of time. Always be thinking of an easier way to get things done. It is not being lazy, it is being smart.

It is estimated that the average sales person spends only about one to two hours of their working time each day actually selling the prospect or customer. One of the largest percentages of time is wasted by calling on customers who are not available at the particular time when the sales person calls.

Use the telephone to call customers and prospects for definite appointments. A few minutes on the phone in the afternoon confirming tomorrow's appointments can be the most productive time spent.

The best way to overcome telephone call reluctance is to have all the calls grouped together and make them all at once. That way if someone turns you down for an appointment, is rude to you, or doesn't give you the business this week, you can move right on to the next call before you have a chance to think about it.

Prospecting by phone differs in the objective you have when you are calling on someone in person. You are not trying to sell your company, products, prices, service, quality or anything, for that matter. The only thing you are trying to sell is an appointment and the only purpose is to get some information.

"Hello, this is Jane Smith with (your company) and we are doing some research on how we might better serve the healthcare industry. Would you be kind enough to schedule a 15 minute appointment for me to ask you a few questions"?

Their possible response: We don't need any more suppliers - we have a contract with.....

"The purpose of my visit is not to try to sell you anything, but simply to ask you some questions, what day do you set aside for appointments? Would 2 o'clock work?

Their possible response might be: I am really pretty busy... I don't have time."

"I will not need more than 15 minutes. Would morning or afternoon work out better for you?"

Comments:

I partially agree with this report in the fact that you can cover a larger area in less time by using the telephone to secure appointments. If I make 30 telephone calls, I may get 2 appointments. But if I make 15 door to door calls in the medium to smaller market area, I usually will get the chance to meet with 6 decision makers enabling me to gather the information I need for a proposal to deliver the next day.

Gregg Nixon

I agree with a majority of what you have said outside of one line, "move right on to the next call before you have a chance to think about it."

I disagree that this is a good idea because if you are selling over the phone albeit appointments or an actual product, if you get shot down and continue to fire through calls with the same strategy, you are missing a key element of selling; learning from your mistakes.

Don't just jump onto the next call yet; ask yourself why they turned you down? Was it legitimate or a smoke screen? Did I ask/say the wrong thing? Was I speaking with the right person in the first place? How can I change the outcome next time?

If you can answer these questions, then move onto the next call and you will be exceedingly more efficient in your daily trials and tribulations.

"The definition of craziness is doing the same thing over and over and expecting a different result."

Joseph Irimescu

In my opinion the sales process has many avenues: phone, email, fax, print (mail) and in person. All have their own merit in a sales process, and all are ways of "touching" your prospect by different means and on a continual basis. The phone aspect needs to be planned, prepared and organized – focused on just getting the appointment. Without a clear plan, phone conversations can be easily diverted. The beauty of the phone portion of your campaign is that rejection is not such a bitter pill – someone says no just click it away and move on to the next possibility.

Danielle Antonacci

Telephone reluctance is hard to handle, the cold call is the drawback of the sales profession. It's is the fear of rejection that intimidates us. You just have to deal with it and move on!

Morgan Frazier

I do not think cold calling on the phone is worthwhile. I do think the phone can be used extensively with clients you have met face to face for setting appointments and maintaining accounts.

An "in person" cold call allows you to get your business card in the customer's hand and get their card. They will remember you on the next call even if you were rejected the first time. I could never be a telemarketer.

Crocker Smith

5. How can you avoid going on the defensive?

A customer's first objective is to take control of the sales person. This is usually accomplished by having a ready-made objection. Try this reverse psychological questioning approach.

Do you know that you can't sell anybody anything! That's right, it can't be done. No one can sell you or me anything we don't want. And if they do, we will more than likely take it back or resent the fact that they persuaded us to buy it in the first place.

No, you can't sell anybody anything, but here is what you can do. And with this concept your life is about to get a whole lot easier. All you have to do is help people make good decisions. And the good decision will be to buy from YOU.

Here's what I mean.

When you go into a computer store to buy software how do you make your decision? You look over the package and read the benefits the software will provide you. You read the problems it will help you solve. And most importantly, you will see a grid with product comparisons. After you study all the information the packaging provides, you make your decision.

Ask yourself this question: Why would someone want to buy products and services from me? Once you have your complete list of benefits you are ready to make your grid, like they do on the software package.

The next step is to take control by approaching your customer with a negative comment. For example, "This product may not be for you."

I know, I know, that is the exact opposite of how you have been taught to sell. But consider this. Regardless of what a sales person says, a customer or prospect has a natural tendency to disagree and gain control of the conversation. By making a negative statement you can actually get a positive response. On the other hand, if we make a positive statement they will respond with a negative statement.

Let me give you a couple of examples and let you decide.

Let's say you are going to help the armed forces recruiting efforts. Their normal approach has been to try and convince someone to join by presenting all the benefits. Here is the negative approach I am talking about:

"The Army may not be for you! Why not get the facts, see if you qualify, and then make a good sound decision as to whether this would be a good career choice."

Do you see the psychology behind this approach?

"The Army may not be for you."

What does that statement provoke? It makes you ask the question: Why not? Why wouldn't it be for me? It makes the prospect wonder what the facts are, what information do they have that will help me make a good decision. It doesn't insult my intelligence by assuming that they know what I want. It lowers the resistance that comes natural when someone is being presented with a sales pitch.

"Why not get the facts."

This implies a "no obligation" investigation into what they have that I might be interested in. It peaks my interest without undue pressure. And it takes much of the pressure off the seller as well. Instead of having the image of a high pressure sales person, the recruiter becomes a career consultant by presenting their facts and using their comparison grid to help the prospect make a good decision.

"See if you qualify."

This provokes a challenge. No one likes to be in a position of not being qualified.

Like a good lawyer, you always want to take control by asking questions that you know what your response will be. Here are a few more examples you can use to test the concept.

How would you answer these negative questions?

Did I catch you at a bad time?

I have a new, high quality product, but you may not want to look at it?

I have three consulting packages, but you may not want to look at the most expensive one?

Comments:

This one is pretty good. When I first read it I thought well that is crazy. Why would you be negative about it. But it made sense when you say this may not be for you the first thing I would think would be well why isn't it for me? What do you know that I don't. It would make you look at it in a different way.

Michelle Jones

I tell my customers frequently that a product may not be right for them, but I mean it. Then I proceed to tell them about the product that is right. This helps build credibility and prevents them from wasting their time and money. My expertise is what they get in addition to the product they purchase.

Danny Swafford

This is an interesting lesson. The statement "See if you qualify "seems to be used a lot by the car dealers this day and age to lure in customer.

I remember selling a used high end amplifier to a guy after I asked him about his related equipment. I made a statement that the amp I had was probably more than he needed. He just had to have it then and bought it [in actuality is was more than he needed with the other components and speakers he had but he had a great amp then to build a better system around.

Cary McAfee

This approach can be successful if it is used in the proper manner and with selected customers. The wording must be to the effect that you do not insult or belittle the customer.

Phil Hackett

When I read this, I envisioned myself saying to a customer..."our service may not be for you". At first, it sounds crazy, but if you think about it, you can spin that statement into a great selling technique. If you follow that up with "Some companies have all the time in the world to recruit and train staff, and they do it right, the first time, every time. However, if your company is not as lucky, let me go over some benefits and see if we might be able to relieve some of your HR and staffing needs.," you might just talk yourself into a deal with a new client.

Laura Czajka

With this type of approach (which I think can be very effective) One has to maintain a level of confidence and word the negative in a very specific way. I like setting the challenge in the example " but you probably do not want to look at the most expensive one " but it could also backfire terribly as your comment could be perceived by the customer as an insult. You could possibly send a message that you believe the customer is " cheap"

I would actually prefer "

I have three quality levels of burgers for you to sample Joe. I know you do not normally buy the higher quality products and if you would rather not invest the money I understand. I can't take it back so try it anyway , I would like your opinion on it in any case.

Alex McQueen

6. When should you deny or admit an objection?

Deny the objection if it is false. Admit the objection if it is true.

To answer an objection by denying it is rarely good practice. A denial is justified, however, If the objection is obviously untrue.

Always enter a denial if the prospect questions your own honesty or integrity or that of your company or any of its management. In such a case you have no alternative but to deny it firmly, since a sales person cannot answer that sort of an objection with arguments, reasons, or talk. Look directly at the prospect, and say slowly and clearly, "I don't believe I quite understand what you say." That gives the prospect a chance to cool down and soften what he says.

Another response might be, "Well, fortunately for me that doesn't happen to be the real story," or "I have some facts that do not altogether agree with what you say." Make it clear to your prospect that you are not intimidated and are ready to proceed with your presentation. Denial is sometimes necessary, even at the loss of a sale. Some sales people have won respect with their customers by becoming known as people who could not be intimidated.

Certain objections to buying cannot be overcome-because they are valid, true, and unanswerable. So admit them and drive on. Don't waste time trying to convince the prospect that he is wrong especially if he isn't. If the prospect says, "I'm overstocked now" - and you know that is the truth - don't get into an argument with him as to whether or not he is overstocked. Instead say, for example, "I know how things are at this time of year. However, I have a couple of items you will want to look at because nobody else in this town is offering them and they have proved to be fast sellers."

Because businesses are more complex, there is more for a sales person to learn about the company. A sales person must know his or her own company's policies on product, terms of sale, delivery and credit. In other words, you must have particular knowledge. In addition, sales people today must know more than merely how to sell; they must know how to sell the products of their particular company.

Whether or not a particular selling task is complex or difficult depends to a considerable extent upon the nature of the product. For example, it is easier to sell a simple, non-technical article whose use is immediately apparent than it is to sell a technical, complicated product that must be described, and the uses ,of which must be explained. It is likewise easier to sell a widely advertised line with an established demand than it is to sell an unknown and unbranded product. Selling is also easier in a market where there is little competition than in one that is highly competitive. You need the skill to handle the particular selling problem presented by the nature of the product which is given to you to sell.

Comments:

I have always maintained that you can't argue or persuade against two things as a salesman, the truth and stupid. If someone is telling you the truth then accept it and move on. If someone has a perception or history with the company that cannot be fixed then thank them and move on. If someone is too blind to look at other options and realize that change is inevitable, move on. You can't fix "stupid". I don't say it lightly - some folks just can't be educated.

Dave Ferren

I feel that you should never tell a client something you can not produce just to tell them what they want to hear. Always be honest and explain whatever objections they might have with the truth. In cases where the objections are not correct explain with honesty and integrity.

Heath Blanchard

Of course you should deny if a statement a client makes is completely untrue, but there definitely is a way to do this tactfully. I have used the statement "I understand" many times when I am trying to build a client relationship. This statement can be used in any situation when a person is frustrated with a specific instance. You can use this in business and on a personal level.

Many times when a client is frustrated they want to vent. Sales people have to realize even if the conversation is a little heated you are still able to turn that around to build on your relationship. At least they are opening up to you, even if it is focused on the negative at times.

Danah Parmley

If you force somebody to buy something they don't want or need, they won't even give you the time of day next time, they will remember the last time you harassed them into a sale. You have lost that customer forever by arguing the point when you just accept it or redirect the objection and possibly just loose the sale instead of the customer.

Morgan Frazier

Objections are one of those things that if its true no matter what you do it will resurface at a later date. But if it's false and you can get the sale. you usually prove it to the customer over a period of time.

Dominick Yarnal

Objections are obviously a natural part of the sales process. But if a customer says he will not buy from you because of poor service or a personality conflict with someone in your company you can use this as an opportunity to create a long term customer by rectifying the situation. If you have a fault and you change for the better people will love you for it.

Crocker Smith

7. "I don't care about anything but price?"

Don't back down when your customer complains about price.

Here is a lesson I learned over 25 years ago that I have never forgot.

Many years ago in a small New England town I owned a meat processing company. I was replacing the freezer compressor and wanted to have a new one installed. I called the top company in the state and a sales person gave me a price.

Then a rival sales person called and offered to do the job for half as much. I phoned the first sales person and told him about the incredible difference in price, and asked how come.

And he told me:

"Many people have gotten into this field recently, They rebuild compressors as a sideline over in the corner of the factory, or in someone's backyard garage. They're cheap all right and 'cheap' is the word. These cheap ones don't run efficiently."

"Your saving in the purchase price would be used up in the first two or three years in the cost of additional electricity. But that's not the half of it. "These half-price compressors keep breaking down-and these companies don't service their products. They don't have the staff to do It. It's disastrous to have your freezer go out in summer weather."

"When you buy a compressor for your company, you've got to buy reliability. Our company is called on to service these cheap compressors . We do what we can with them after we take care of our regular customers. Many of the buyers of these cheap compressors, after a couple of years of headaches, switch over to one of our systems."

"Why not start with one of our compressors? You'll be ahead in actual costs in no time at all. You'll be ahead In having an efficient and virtually trouble-free system. You'll have a top cooling system by a top company that serves 80% of the people in this area-and we're known for our fast response to every call for help."

I bought the higher priced compressor from this "Cutting Edge" sales person who told me with irrefutable logic why I should buy from him, and I was never sorry. I needed one repair in 5 years and the repair man was there in half an hour.

You can do the same thing when a customer tells you that your price is too high, or a competitor called and said they could it for much less. The key is to know your product inside and out. Know the business environment the you work in and continuously be on the lookout for points of interest and points of difference that will keep you in tune with what's going on in your marketing area.

Comments:

Many times it is the new business owner who goes for the lowest price. I try to give them names and numbers of our established customers that have tried the lowball outfit and experienced the difference in quality and service. Once again, an unbiased opinion can make a deal work for you.

Crocker Smith

The lesson, again, is that "you get what you pay for" …. We have a couple competitors in town who like to purport that they are less expensive than us. They obviously don't know how we bill our clients. We have an all inclusive rate. If there was a situation that required us to have add-on charges, we make it absolutely clear to our clients up front.

One of our competitors undercut our markups at one of our clients. They said they could offer a lower rate than we charged. Our client took the bait, only to find out when they received the invoice that there were several extraneous fees, to include a mysterious "administration fee" and mailing fees and they billed extra for drug screens. All in all our customer would have gotten better, more honest service from us. We didn't need to tell them that, they vowed never to use the competition again. The fact of the matter is that we are worth it.

If a customer simply won't budge on your lowest acceptable rate, well, on to the next! No point in lowering your price to put yourself in a position where you might lose money.

Marquesa Ortega

People that say all they care about is price must have a fleet of people ready to help for free! The fact is, once we find them a top grade product with top grade performance, our clients will certainly expect top grade service if and when this time comes - and why not, they paid for it. If they buy bargains, they get bargains, and bargain service to go along with it.

I know of some DIY kind of proprietors here in town, and they claim to be able to fix, repair, install, and operate everything in their establishment. This certainly is a point of pride for many owners. In practice - these same people are very overworked, and it shows when it comes to PR related issues. Spread yourself too thin, and you burn out.

When you buy the top grade from us, you get our team's knowledge, expertise, and we will ensure your service needs are met. By realizing better efficiency in electrical power, smoother operation at all times, and higher resale values of the equipment, the upfront costs are quickly offset, and once the clients get a taste of the performance and service, they don't go back to entry level - I'd ask the price client - EVER WONDER WHY??

Wendy Parrott

About the author Bob Oros

Regardless of whether you are reading one of his books or attending one of his programs, the most frequent comment is: "This guy has been there, he is one of us, I am going to use these strategies."

With over 2,000 speaking engagements in all 50 states and several international locations for manufacturers, distributors and associations, you can be sure you will get the results and information you are looking for. Prior to starting his speaking career, Bob served six years in the US Navy as a Communications Specialist and then worked his way from a street sales person to the position of National Sales Manager for a Fortune 200 company.

Bob has received awards for speaking, writing and marketing too numerous to mention.

Additional Topics by Bob Oros

Why Sales People Fail

The Key to Selling Anybody

The Power of Expectations

Add Value to Every Product

How to Justify Your Price

Lost in 60 Seconds

One Good Reason to Buy

Control a Buyer's Attitude

How to Create Demand

Smoke Screen Objections

Take the Risk Out of Sales

How Small Companies Get Big

www.ingramcontent.com/pod-product-compliance
Lightning Source LLC
Chambersburg PA
CBHW030010190526
45157CB00015B/2205